Dragon Breath

A BOOK OF POETRY

Poetry by
Lynn Meador

Dragon Breath

Copyright © 2023 by Lynn Meador

All rights reserved. No part of this publication may be reproduced, distributed, or transmitted in any form or by any means, including photocopying, recording, or other electronic or mechanical methods, without the prior written permission of the copyright holder, except in the case of brief quotations embodied in critical reviews and certain other noncommercial uses permitted by copyright law. For permission requests, write to the publisher, addressed "Attention: Permissions Coordinator," at the address below.

ISBN: 978-1-64318-114-1

703 Eighth St.
Baldwin City, KS, 66006
www.imperiumpublishing.com

Dragon Breath

A BOOK OF POETRY

IMPERIUM PUBLISHING
CREATE YOUR STORY

Poetry by
Lynn Meador

This is my truth.

Reader, please understand —
My truth is intertwined
With the other actors in my story
But is not necessarily the same.

I was taught that
Truth will set you free,
And that freedom is good.
So this is my truth,
And only mine.

Author's note: These pieces were written over a number of years, in numerous small towns across the US. Although none of these words are fiction, they may be dramatized in an attempt to express the author's emotions, sometimes spanning decades and multiple types of life experiences. Please accept these words for what they are — raw musings on life, in non-chronological order

Bareback

Dark
Warm summer breeze
Sand whispers under pony feet
Brown eyes, skin, hair
Invisible

Free
Bareback, clinging
Hands tangled, fistfuls of mane
Wild, untamed, racing
Headstrong

Time
Heartbeat thudding
Star studded Nebraska sky
Poverty, loss, abuse
Forgotten

Pain
Baggage left behind
Eclipsed in ecstatic thrill
Bodies in sync
Riding free

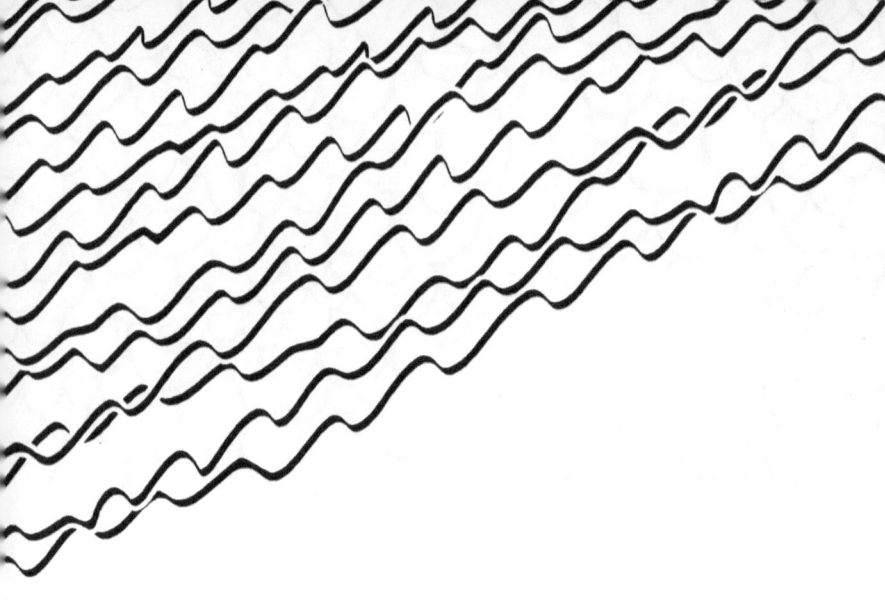

Breathing Fire

My friend asked: "If you say that forfeiting your own voice is the lesser of two evils, what is the first evil, the worst one? and to whom is it the lesser of two evils?"

The first evil is alienating everyone and everything I've ever cared about. I've stayed silent my entire life to keep the peace because it doesn't hurt anyone but me.

It's the lesser of two evils for my husband, my birth family, the church world. They don't want to deal with me as a non-Christian, non-conservative female with opinions. Most of my friends are my friends anyway, no matter what I say or believe. For some reason, I've shared much with friends that I never could with family.

It was the lesser of two evils for me as a child, because I got punished less than the other kids. I was quiet, reserved. Shy, they said. My words were wrapped around my heart and throat, choking and squeezing, keeping me from verbalizing even if I wanted to.

But keeping them inside also protected me. It was a wall around my mind that allowed me to think taboo thoughts, dream taboo dreams. I was able to model the expected life on the outside, avoid a lot of the punishment, and still protect my mind. It kept the stinging criticism and rejection on the outside and allowed me to be a real person inside.

I know the term for this is probably dissociation. I've always been able to separate myself, as if I were standing apart, watching myself think. Choosing my responses based on what would be the least disruptive to everyone else—cause the least possible conflict and pain.

No one knew. Maybe my cousin knew a little? He was the only one who saw inside at all, and I never fully trusted him, even though he was my best friend.

Today, right now, forfeiting my voice is still a protective mechanism for me, to keep at bay the critical voices that can drown me purely in sheer numbers.

If I had the ability to breathe fire, I might feel the same need to forfeit my voice in order to protect those around me. There's a chance that a fire breather who holds the fire inside always would eventually incinerate. Here's to learning to breathe fire, as gently as possible.

Fire

I was six. Early spring in the northern woods. It was cold, and I had on a long nightgown. In my mind, it's shapeless and colorless. But it came to my feet.

I don't really remember her waking us up, just her telling the story. I remember hearing the smoke alarms. I remember seeing the fire in the addition Dad had built as we walked past. King, our golden retriever, was in Dad's old red Jeep—jumping over the seats, barking like crazy. He felt trapped. So did I.

I watched him from someplace else. Someplace far away. I thought he would die. I thought the fire would get the Jeep too. I don't know where our Collie was. Maybe she was far enough away in her kennel that dad left her there?

I remember the trucks. I remember the fire—bright orange-red in the middle of the night. The flames were so tall I couldn't see the stars. Surrealistically tall pine trees all around, engulfing, watching. I was afraid the whole forest would burn.

There were hoses all across our yard, and the lights and fire made it bright as day. We kids were in the green 69 Chevy Impala. I don't think we could have had it very long yet, a hand-me-down from Dad's grandmother.

It was so, so cold. My sister was screaming, my brother was freaking out about everything he knew was burning. And I was silent. I was dreaming. I wanted to wake up.

I don't remember going to Grandma's house. I remember waking up on her living room floor, smelling of smoke and coughing. I remember my auntie bathing me and cutting down some of her clothes for me so she could wash my nightie. It was all I had.

There was a giant hole in the back of the trailer, where our room was. It was blackened, still smoldering when we went over the next day. It wasn't real, it couldn't be. My mind restarted with a blank slate. That whole summer is mostly gone, even though I usually remember everything.

I remember seeing plastic melted into weird shapes, silverware twisted and melted into lumps. Odd bits and pieces of things that survived. All my clothes were gone, of course. It's all that mattered to me.

People brought us car loads and bags of food, clothes, dishes, linens, everything we could possibly need. I don't remember ever feeling like I owned my own clothing again, until I was an adult. We lived that summer in a travel trailer at Grandma's house.

I know my brother fell off the top bunk and cut his head open to the bone. I was there. I don't remember it.

There were crocks of cucumbers pickling in a screen tent. My cousin and I playing to our hearts' content. I was afraid of several extended family members, but I loved my cousin and auntie and grandma. There was summer produce in the garden, pulling weeds in the mornings and "picking potato bugs" with Grandma. Berry picking in the woods. Cherry orchards.

Then it got cold again, and Mom and Dad still didn't have a place for us to live on my birthday. The weekend jaunts with the little trailer into the woods had to stop. Eventually they bought a new mobile home, mainly through a charity loan.

I remember watching the trucks park it in the mobile home park. I remember the skirting and the steps. There were neighbors all around, and I felt naked. Exposed. I'd never lived close to people I didn't know.

Later on, there was a trailer close enough to ours I could touch both trailers ... as a 10 year old.

I remember it was almost Thanksgiving, and I was curled up asleep over a register, trying to stay warm, in a still-empty trailer. It was ours, and it was new. We were so proud. All five of us.

I was 18 when I moved into a non-trailer home for the first time. My husband and I bought our first home when I was 30. It was concrete, and so solid.

He never understood why I insisted on fire alarms. This is why. They saved my life, somehow, when I was six. I would have melted like the wall did.

I remembered most of this, for the very first time, the summer my family became houseless and I moved my 1 & 5-year-old daughters into a borrowed travel trailer with my husband. I had nightmare flashbacks with excruciating details for a week. Tonight, I remembered more due to a work event that triggered some memories.

Human pacifier

1969 Chevy Impala
double bench seats.
Me,
in the middle.
Always in the middle.

Keeping my brother
away from my sister
Keeping my sister from screaming and hitting my brother.
I could take their bullshit and stop it, so I sat in between.

Pileup.
Memories in the car
late at night.
Brother against the door,
My head on him,
my sister on me.
Warm and safe,
sleep.

My body
always in the middle.
A human pacifier,
so those in my life
could sleep.

Dreams

Floating away
Bubbles in the wind
Large, small, iridescent

Innocence
Chasing, racing, hoping
All is possible, now

Wistful
Face upturned
Disappointed eyes tracing

Spheres
Ethereal, temporal
More myth than truth

Restless Grief

Encroaching darkness
Fire sky edging black thunderheads
Storms gathering, restless
Ready to unleash fury

Breathless pain
One year gone
Tragedy tore open my scars
Exposed my naked soul

Now—worldwide grief
Keening, wailing, traumatic waves
Bodies lie stacked
Unburied or too hastily done

A nation struggles to accept
To believe in reality
Eyes closed to facts
Grasping conspiracy

Familiar grief, ignored
Generations of pain
Buried deep inside
In the name of strength

I see dead people

When I watched The Sixth Sense, I knew intuitively how it would end. I've been Cole my whole life. Obviously not literally ... but I see pain, I feel it. It rips me apart. And I'm every bit as afraid as he was. Cole is a young boy with a scary gift, the ability to see dead people as if they're alive.

I want very much to write how this makes me feel. I've been staring at my screen forever, trying to get some words out. Sometimes words are such a terrible vehicle for communication.

If I allow myself, I can feel other people's pain & trauma so deeply it wounds me, even traumatizes me. This has always been true. It's part of me.

It comes out in strange ways sometimes. Knowledge that something will happen before it does, based on the emotional dynamics. I have dreams that tell me true stories about people, that must come out of my subconscious because they're not based on conscious knowledge.

Traumatic injury and death, suicide, grief of all sorts ... They wrap around my heart until I can't breathe. After my reservation years, I turned most of that part of my soul off as much as I could. I avoided homeless people, tried not to think of poverty, hunger, raw pain. Yes I know—there's so much inherent privilege in that statement.

The hundreds of traumatic deaths and suicides of my childhood and teen years—deaths of people I knew, families I interacted with regularly—were tattooed on my soul. All of it's still there inside me: Abused children, desperate for kindness & love. Hungry eyes, eyeing the snacks I passed out.
It's not the physical pain that destroys me most. It's the fear, anger, grief writ large in faces too old for small bodies. Or middle-aged people with deep grief lines, doing the best they can to care for their family. Grieving daily, because life is pain.

There's the torture in a mother's eyes at the wake of her 18-year-old son's funeral. She found him in the garage, the week before Christmas. They were drinking together the night before, and he hung himself after an argument with her. She never forgave herself. I remember the emptiness in her eyes years later.

A whole town keening the suicide of an 11-year-old, gone quietly when no one was paying attention. Grandmothers, fearing for their grandchildren, unable to keep them safe.

There are the adult eyes of a 10-year-old, forever part of my soul. He watched me, the 14 or 15-year-old in charge of children's services, to be sure the little ones were safe with me. His name was Justin. He had a heart shaped face and a soul of fire and warmth.

I watched him brood over the others, and stop the bullies from hurting the babies. I watched him share his snacks, candy, prizes even. If I believe human nature can be good, it's because of Justin.

He died when he was 14, on a drunken joyride with his cousin. It's been 20 years, and I've never forgotten. His eyes haunt me. He was tough as nails on the outside, and broken as I was on the inside.

I don't tell these stories, because no one would believe it. Also because they still hurt, and I don't want anyone else to carry them.

When I was 11, I opened the door to find a man who was a family friend standing there covered in blood. He'd been in a brawl with his brother. We found out later the brother nearly died.

I cope very, very well in emergencies. My mind goes into a calm, logical mode that works perfectly for triage and damage control.

After, I shatter.

I could honestly tell stories all day. Many of them are much, much worse. I used to think PTSD was for people who went to war and saw horrible things. It is, of course.

But I've seen dead people too.

They haunt me.

I still feel the weight of their dreams, their lives, their nightmares, their hope.

Whatever this gift or curse I have is, I want to use it to help hurting people. But first I have to help myself—which is so much harder to do than it seems.

There are those I love trapped in a third dimension of pain and grief. I will find a way to help, to heal. To make others whole. I just need to do it safely, without destroying myself in the process.

I'm working on that.

mirror eyes

Dead pools
unplumbed depths
of pain.
Falling,
dizzy,
invisible

Dull green
shadowland
rivers
of tears
wasted,
bone dry.

Flatline
don't feel
shrink,
smaller yet,
inside...
iced fire.

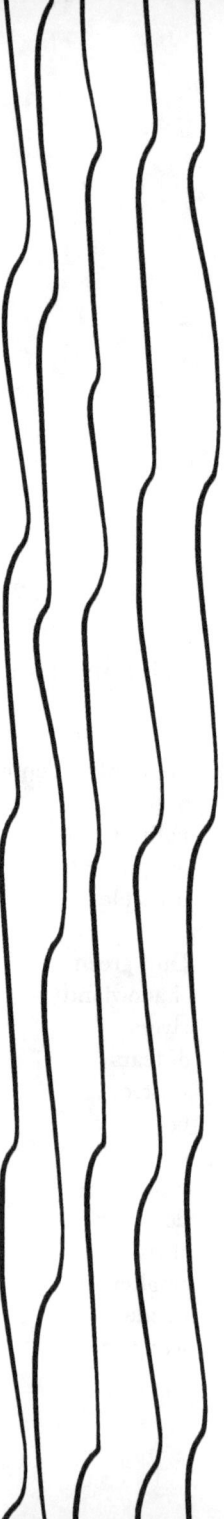

last days

Paper thin skin
Waiting for
Death
To end life
Again

Bodies suspend
Waiting for
Life
To begin
And end

Scorching hot hand
Knowing it
Ends
And still
Reaching for more

ghosts

Sleeping with the light on
Because I don't believe in god
But I still believe in ghosts

I don't trust the dark
Or myself
Or my dreams
Not tonight
Not now

God was my Ivanhoe

You know that feeling when you've used prayer as an alternative to working out the really big problems your entire life? Then you lose any and all real belief in prayer, or a divine deity who is omniscient, omnipotent, ominous, or whatevs ... Something happens ...

Something or someone you care about goes sidewise, you feel desperately inadequate and want to cry out to a higher power. And there's nothing.

You can't even form words without ridiculing yourself, it's so silly.

God was my Ivanhoe.
My white knight.
The being who allowed me to be weak, be a damsel in distress in need of salvation. I'm not riffing on Christianity as a whole here. I'm just trying to explain what happened to
me, how my life and my heart suddenly has an omnipresent hole in it.

Relationships & communicating are hard work when you're no longer expecting some other being to swoop in and save the day by reframing the conflict or beating the other person into your mold.

Hatred, meekness, humility, servanthood, anger and forgiveness (to name a few) also take on a different connotation.

They are no longer mandated by an omniscient, omnipresent being who will be angry if you fuck up and show your humanity accidentally.

Actually, they're not mandated at all.

If you're angry, frustrated, sad, raging, hating someone, even proud or jealous ... Who knew?? They're human emotions.

Denying them doesn't erase them. It just takes away all possibility that you could respond to them appropriately.

I'm facing down what feels like an impossible wind tunnel of emotions. Or maybe a wormhole.

My entire life was based on a construct I no longer see as valid, and now find harmful.

Allowing pain and fear to escape their prison allowed a gap big enough for rage and hate also. I'm pretty sure this is a healthy development, but it hurts like hell.

Especially when I'm able to move past the protection of anger and can feel the loss and fear.

I no longer trust myself and my memories of pretty much any relationship, situation, or event that happened pre-deconstruction. There's too much bullshit, too much fog.

Too much blind gratitude for being allowed to exist.

Monster

Monster
In the dark
Under the bed
Downstairs
Behind the door

Hideous
Terrorizing us all
Nameless
Faceless
Frankenstein

Its name
My name
They are the same
I am afraid
Of myself

Dragon Breath

wind-up toy

Drained...
Of words
Energy
Resources
Emotion

I feel like a wind-up toy with a broken part.
I'm still whirring but nothing's moving.

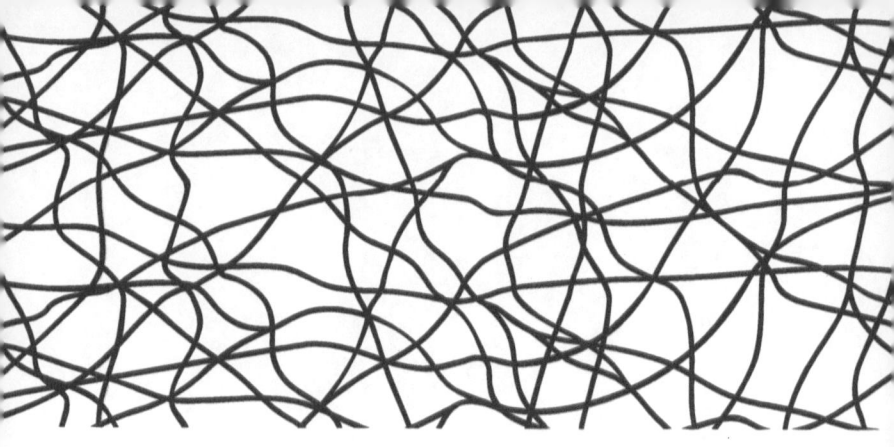

Counting the Cost

What happens when you walk away from nearly four decades of a highly conservative church world that is your birthright? When your truth and need to survive finally surmount the desire for safety? Here are a few of the issues I faced.

The social and logistical costs are staggering.
- Complete career inadequacy.
- No safety net.
- Friendships that are not just gone but craters in the ground.
- Zero network outside church circles because you're not allowed.
- Meaningless degrees, because how do you make a living with a degree in "missions" or "Bible?"

I was far more fortunate than many. In the world I came from, living space is often tied to church and school jobs. In 2016, for the first time in my life, I navigated a normal rent market.

My parents very nearly ended up living on the streets after a school kicked them out.

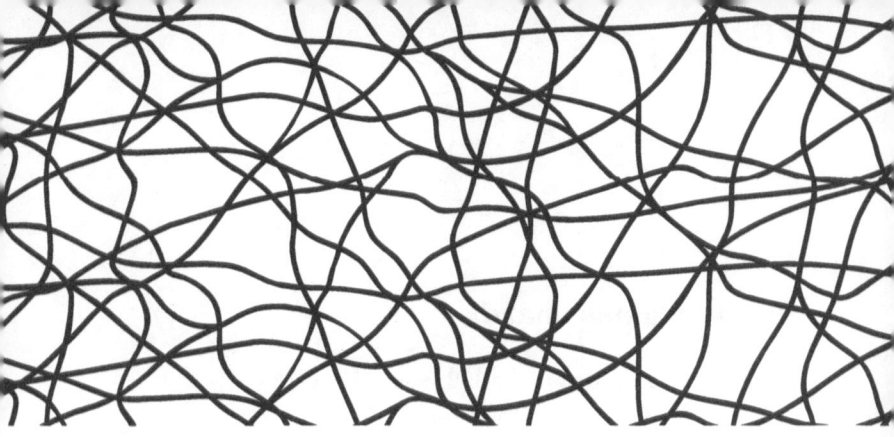

The emotional costs are devastating.
Leaving a strict evangelical church is often the equivalent of burning everything you own and trying to start over with no family, no friends, no job, and no marketable skills. It takes time, enormous amounts of energy, and incredible willpower.

On top of that, you have the knowledge that everyone in your old world thinks you're eternally damned and hopeless.

Maybe the strangest part: Everyone thinks you took the easy way out.
Your old friends—because you left the straight and narrow, because broad is the path that leads to destruction.
Everyone else—because they don't understand how you could live the way you did in the first place.

Stained glass shards

Stained glass windows, in a 100-year-old church
Lit from inside on a midweek night.
I leave my front door, needing air, space, time to breathe free.
The church windows glimmer across the street, beckoning with
layers of history, ritual, and a familiar culture.

I turn away ...

Not because I hate.
Not because I don't want to belong.
Not even because I don't believe.

I move on, not knowing for sure where I'm going.
Knowing I need to go.
Certain truth is real and solid.
Believing truth will set me free.

Truth is not inside church walls.
It's not bound inside stained glass windows and fancy crosses.
Truth is around, inside, above and below.

Truth is knowing what is real.
Avoiding what is not.
Allowing pain for the sake of wholeness.

Truth is found in freedom.
In honest living.

And God?

He is truth.
He is not bound by time …
Walls.
Ritual.
Rules.

God is truth, freedom, love.
He is air and breath.
He does not call to fear, but to life.

1am on the clock

Shattered glass—
A nation awake
1 AM on the clock
A million years
To morning, ffs

Shattered glass—
The state
Our hearts
Our nation
Our souls

Shattered glass—
The bodies
Sick, dying, dead
Friends, lovers
Mothers, fate

Shattered glass.
In god we trust
Except
Who is He
To inspire such hate?

written at 1am on January 7th, 2021

Dragon Breath

no rest

No rest for the wicked
they said
Weary souls going to hell
deservedly

No rest for the victims
~yet~
we said
Weary souls going to heal
defiantly

Women aren't funny

"Your wife must have a sense of humor. She's seen you naked." - The Marvelous Mrs. Maisel

I'm neither Jewish nor a comedian.
My family is deeply evangelical for generations—Pastors, teachers, missionaries. I grew up on a mission field. I didn't expect The Marvelous Mrs. Maisel to hit me between the eyes.

When I was 16, I told my father I wanted to be a lawyer and maybe a politician. He thought that was a great idea. He's always said I was smart, and encouraged me to go to college.

But he had no resources to give—neither financial nor practical. And when I graduated from high school, I did not have the ability to seek out a school, scholarships, etc.

By then, I'd been indoctrinated in the idea that it's pure folly for anyone—particularly a girl!—to attend secular university. You would simply be throwing away your faith. God can't bless that ... so I let go of the dream.
Now it's back.

I thought I had dealt with all my issues with ultra-conservative evangelicalism. I didn't think it affected me anymore. I've changed. Intellectually, logically, practically, maybe even spiritually—it doesn't really affect my actual thinking processes anymore.

I've intentionally forgiven dozens upon dozens of individual people, and the entire church/ school/ culture system that caused immeasurable harm to my entire family.

But for the first time in my life, I'm stepping into territory that the entire evangelical ecosystem I grew up in does not approve of—namely, women in professional careers.

I've been a musician, a teacher, a secretary, a home organizer, a caregiver, a bookkeeper, and a stay-at-home mom. All of those things fall within the realm of acceptable things a woman can do. I mean, a woman is naturally good at nurture and support, right? So it's logical.

Now I work with things like economic impact, analytics, workforce development, and community building. Not to mention the teaching and consulting—business planning, marketing strategy, data gathering, and cross-platform content development and strategy.

I mean, sure, I put that stuff in layman's terms as much as possible. But that's what it is. My small town is predominantly a male-run city. Nearly every day, we are made aware of sub-status as women.

My dream is back.
Kind of.

I get to be smart if I can, dig into research and resources, crunch numbers and data, and lead with strategy and marketing ability. I get to allow the geek in me to run absolutely wild and create products I've envied.

I have an opportunity right now to teach people I care a lot about. To help small town business owners get it right, and find resourceful and creative ways to win when the odds are stacked against them. Even revitalize entire communities over time.

I want to make a difference.
Is it just a dream? Maybe women really can't be funny.

deconstruction

Autumn rain
Is deconstruction

An end, not a beginning
Necessary, cleansing
Painfully cold

Tears of pain
Regret
Outside, looking in

Needing more
Missing then

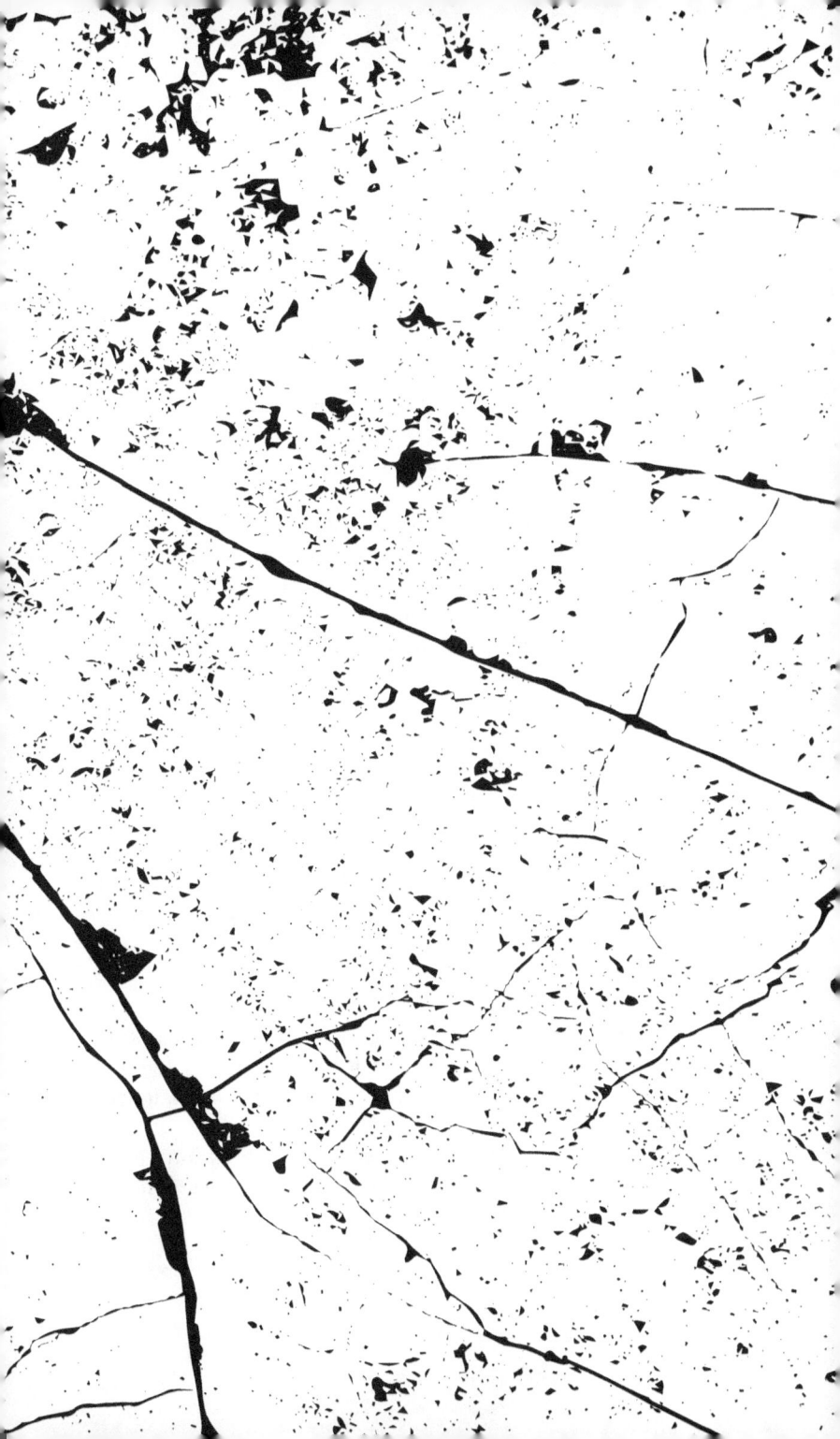

Kaleidoscope

"The only one I rarely feel is anger."
My therapist gave me a chart of emotions, a wheel with labels to help me pinpoint the whirlwind of feelings inside me.

It's useful. If I start with the big primary emotion in the middle and then move out, I can usually land on something that begins to describe how I feel—at least as a jumping off point. And because I'm a nerd, I immediately looked up emotion wheels and discovered there are tons of versions of this.

The Junto Institute even created their own gorgeous version, with as few negative emotions as possible. It's brilliant if you just need a word to get through a team-building exercise. And the range of suggested words is helpful. It just annoys me that they felt scientific models were just too negative and felt a need to add in as many positive words as possible.

So far, Plutchik's circumplex model is the one I like most. It was his theory that these "primary" emotions are bipolar—equal but opposite. The range and possibilities in this model fascinate me.

Anyway, anger. We were talking about my emotions at my last therapy session, and she asked me which emotions I've been able to pinpoint in my journaling.

Here's the strange thing—everything except anger.
I almost never feel anger.
I feel everything—literally everything—else. And, mind you, that's an improvement. A few years ago, I felt like a wooden soldier. Nothing scratched the surface, nothing came out. I was a fortress.

I have so many triggers that make me want to retreat into the silent fort. It's lonely and scary, but it keeps everyone around me safe from my pain.

I struggle with sharing my feelings, my emotion, taking a chance of wounding anyone else. Allowing myself to feel forces the need for me to communicate with humans around me, humans online, humans who've written or created things I want to understand.

And still, I can't feel the anger, except when I think or talk about church issues and spiritual abuse. It's the one major thing in my life that I've dealt with enough times, for enough years, that I have a little bit of distance and perspective. The one thing I sometimes think I have wisdom and understanding about.

I've unconsciously used that anger as a shield for ... maybe most of my life? I remember feeling rage at the mission board my parents worked for. I didn't feel anything at all towards my parents for exposing me to extreme violence and graphic, nightmarish scenarios. I don't even think it occurred to me.

I felt anger towards the school that dumped my parents out of their house into the street with almost no notice. When your job and income are tied to your housing, you have no security at all. I don't remember feeling fear for them (I no longer lived at home at that point). Just a lot of raging, white hot anger.

Anger is one of my motivators. I can move mountains when I'm angry. I talked my mother through the steps to purchase a house when she had almost no options. Helped her secure labor to make the place livable. Personally beat down a wall to open up an old door. And that's another story, but that's how I met my husband.

Anyway.

Today I'm stuck in a kaleidoscope. An emotional vortex inside a hurricane. It's not a good place to be, but it's better than it was. And far better than the options.

Validity

Nobody—and I mean mf nobody—gets to tell me when it's time for me to quit grieving or get over something that hurt me.

I DO NOT CARE what they think they know about it.

It took me a full YEAR of therapy to even think those words.

I'm fully aware that my trauma, my pain, my issues, are not even remotely the worst in the world. THEY ARE STILL VALID.

Don't wanna listen? Then put the book down. My pain is not your burden, not yours to carry. I don't want to hurt others with my words. Ever.

Want to hurt me? Tell me I'm hurting people. And then act like I don't care. My pain and hurt, my emotions, are just as valid as anyone else's.

I am not less than you for any reason whatsoever. I'm not more than you either. I'm just me, and I'm goddamn human. I make mistakes. I am wrong. Often. And I can't always fix shit.

But I CAN try again, and the forces of hell aren't enough to stop me.

I learned when I was teaching that in a child's world, every day is a brand new day. You can have a horrific day in the classroom, and start fresh the next morning. Adulting ain't quite like that.

But I can do better, be better. I don't have to disown or ignore my pain and hurt to do so. I don't have to reduce myself to groveling, and I won't.

Some things are right and true and good, some are not. It's not the same for everyone. I stand in my own truth, goddammit.

limbo

Sleepless
Too hot
Too cold
Bored
Anxious

All the things
Mingling, swirling
Tapping on my brain
Muscles tense

Sleep
Is not sweet
But better than this state
Of limbo

dark

dark, not mere absence of light
entity in its own right
tangible
present
felt
dense,
obscuring my soul

Dust in the wind

Nearly 40 years of life gone.

Everything I've ever done, mountains I've climbed, walls I've broken down ... it feels so pointless.

Ashes, scattered in a flowing river.
Defying my attempts to gather pieces together and find meaning. Words have been my drug of choice for as long as I can remember.

I was two and a half when I was diagnosed with a "minor" hearing loss. 30% on one side, 50% on the other. It's not crippling.

But when you miss roughly one third of each verbal interaction, your brain has to work triple overtime to fill in the blanks.

I had hearing aids for most of my childhood, but they're not always helpful.

My freedom came in the form of written words. First reading, then writing. And in the age of digital communications, meaningful and personal interaction suddenly lost the barrier of hearing loss. Words matter.

And though written words are their own curse sometimes—misunderstandings abound, clarity can be difficult—not having a hearing barrier is freedom.

Train Wreck

You're lashed to the front of a speeding freight train, nothing to protect you from the elements as you race down the track.

The landscape is flying by so fast you can barely identify landmarks as they slide past. It's scary, nauseating, and a bit exciting.

You're not sure where you're going, and the engine behind you isn't giving up secrets.

But for now, it's sunny and pleasant, the landscape is open, the track's flat, and you can see for miles.

So you give in to the excitement and adrenaline rush, and just enjoy the ride.

Soon, the engine you're strapped to comes to a steep incline, and starts down. You start to panic as you realize the dilemma you're in.

You can't move, you can't even put your hands in front of your face, and you can't stop or
control the train.

Fear grips your heart, icy and painful. Your breathing is shallow as the train races into the valley, and you can't see past a steep curve.

Suddenly you're plunged into the inky blackness of a tunnel, and something smashes next to your face.

You strain to see ahead, then close your eyes in the horror of blackness, hoping you'll wake up from this nightmare. The engine races on, unfeeling, uncaring, in a hurry to get wherever it's going.

You have no clue what the destination is, and you're hoping and praying you'll live long enough to get there.

Then the train emerges from the tunnel, out into a mountain meadow. There are wildflowers and birds, beauty everywhere.

The engine can't stop, racing into time.

By now, you don't know whether to be glad you've made it this long or pray something, anything, will stop this. Even a train wreck.

You can't stop, can't get the engine's attention. You have this odd feeling he's enjoying himself, likes speeding into the unknown.

As storm clouds tower ahead and mountain tracks trace into the distance, you realize your proximity to this iron horse will not save you. In actual fact, it's killing you.

You need a break, and there's no brake ...

just do

Numb.
Going through the motions,
just breathing.

I don't feel much these days.
Don't think,
don't feel,
don't speak.
Just do.

safety

What is trust?
What is safety?
What is strength?
Does it take bravery to trust someone who's hurt you or is that stupidity? Safety is relative. There's always an element of risk. How do you know the risk element is too ... risky?

Powerlessness

"It's in defining the dark we learn to understand the light."
Reflecting on what I wrote, I find there's a good bit of this that reminds me how much I've changed, and a good bit that reminds me I haven't at all. I still want good to win. I want to vanquish darkness and pain. I want to heal and bind up. I do believe with all my heart that growth requires community.

I don't believe in God.
I do believe in vulnerability.
I don't have faith in institutions.
I do have faith in imperfect goodness.
I think perhaps the church as a whole has one thing right: We all seek community.
I wrote the words below before I left the church.

A culture of powerlessness.
Doing what we're told.
Needing experts to explain everything to us.

Am I talking American politics or the church world?
You decide.

I think it's both, and I've got stuff to say.

On an intensely personal level, I'm struggling with corruption right now.

Political
Church
Corporate
Interpersonal
Community

I'm an idealist at heart, and in my mind I'm Frodo. If I can succeed in destroying the heart of evil, good will flourish.

I'm hating church more and more every week. I feel like it's every church everywhere, and it hurts.

I believe in God.
I believe He is good.
I don't believe in the same God I grew up with, who was demanding and abusive.

I want to believe good will always win over evil.
I used to believe church corruption was mostly within the small, cultish circles I moved in. It's not true.
The evil feels bigger and uglier now.

Community is essential for anyone who wants to grow and become a better person.
But many American institutions of church—with all their rituals and demands—are almost inherently counter to biblical teaching.

What the apostles taught—truly—was neighborliness.
Community of friendship.
Coming alongside, working together, teaching and growing together. Not an institution of power, which demands a number of powerless individuals. Power corrupts.

Current research says the brain literally changes with high levels of power. Idolizing pastors—choosing to believe blindly because they are called or ordained of God—puts lay people in extreme danger of exploitation.

This is also true in the political realm, obviously.
And it's interrelated. Many Trump followers believe He is God's chosen.
As such, every word from his mouth is gospel. He can't be wrong: it is God speaking through him.
And if God only speaks through His chosen, we need not exercise our own brains. Or, you know, research.
Or even, God forbid, decide for ourselves who to vote for.
Someone wiser and more in tune with all the intricacies of politics will put out a voters' guide.

I'm finding myself more triggered in everyday life than I ever thought possible.
The church world is supposed to be safe. Just as the Fellowship were supposed to be Frodo's friends and allies.
But it turns out we all have a choice—what to do with the time we are given. We're allowed to choose good or evil.

You can say the universe allows us to choose, or you can say God allows free will. It's all the same from where I'm sitting.
Right now, I'm exploring the darkness. Trying to understand my past in the hope it will shed light on the future.

Because it's in defining the dark that we learn to understand the light.

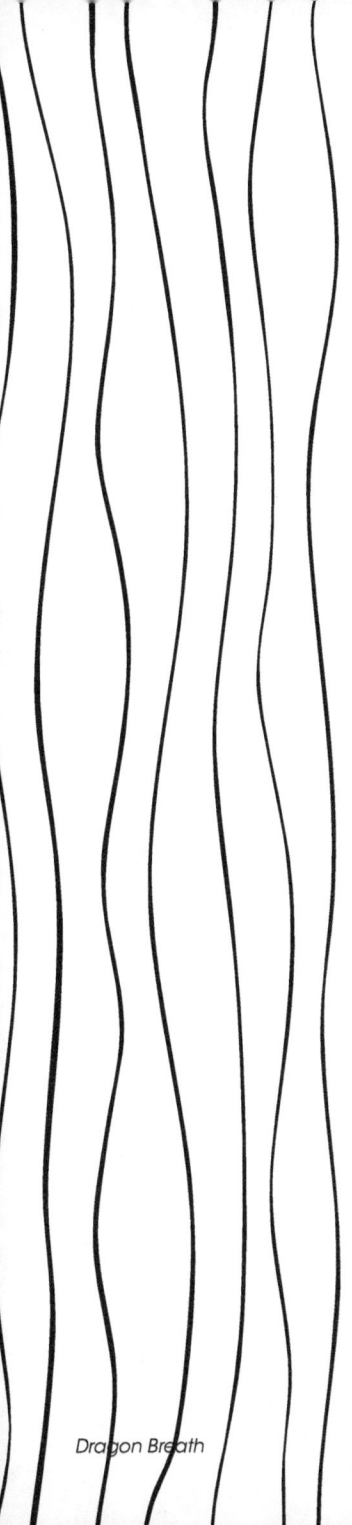

betrayal

Quiet, inside my head
Blankets wrapped tight
Closed eyelids see all
What is safety?
Who cares?
Live, breathe, exist
Mephistopheles
Demands his due
Prince of demons
Condescending laughter
Rage explodes
Fiery sparks lick high
Then
Ashes

Betrayal and anger

What happens when someone has intentionally and repeatedly wronged and harmed you under the guise of friendship for years ... and you know they're an empty shell inside, you know their hurt intimately. But then the tables turn and you're the one with the power to hurt.

Like tectonic plates, shifting, grinding, inexorable but painfully slow, life comes full circle. Revenge is off the table.

Forgiveness doesn't erase pain and a need for closure, nor is forgiveness mandated. For the first time ever, all emotions are valid.
Learning to let go. Allowing my own humanity, as well as theirs.
Refusing to be the B team.

Growth hurts. Change is ugly sometimes.

Anger is justified.
It's protection from the true depth of betrayal underneath, but it doesn't allow forward motion. But anger as an emotion isn't necessarily negative, and I wish I felt it more often. Especially in circumstances where I was truly a victim.

impossible trust

Dragonfly wings
Tiny, impossible, gossamer
Brushing the surface
Skimming away
Nearly invisible

Fragile flight
Iridescent power
Magical moment
Crushed, torn, bruised
Mired in pride

dragon breath

Walking in the dark
Listening to the heartbeat of another tiny town
Drinking in smoky dragon breath.

I wish my nose wasn't so cold
And the funeral parlor downtown
Didn't feel so familiar.
Pausing by the train tracks
Shaking with anger, pain, sadness
That won't be denied.

I wonder briefly why people put blue lights on porches
Cross the street to avoid that mutt
Glance at Joe's new car
Wondering if he remembered to pay the rent.

Skraggly skeleton trees stretch
Scratch my face
Broken limbs from that ice storm
Tripping my feet.

Every story has a moral
Each lyric has a rhyme
Except mine.

Lacking rhyme & reason
Dark seeps into my bruised soul
Freezing my mind
Into painful shapes and shades.

Rules
Laws
Structure
They make life easy.
Defining God
Goodness
Morality.

Subjective truth
Burning outward
From the soul itself
Defies definition.

There's the crossing bell
Warning of danger
Freight train barreling through
Owning the road
Owning the town
Briefly.

The danger passes
Leaves only the menace
Of normalcy
Time
Unhurried
Rushing
Burying me alive.

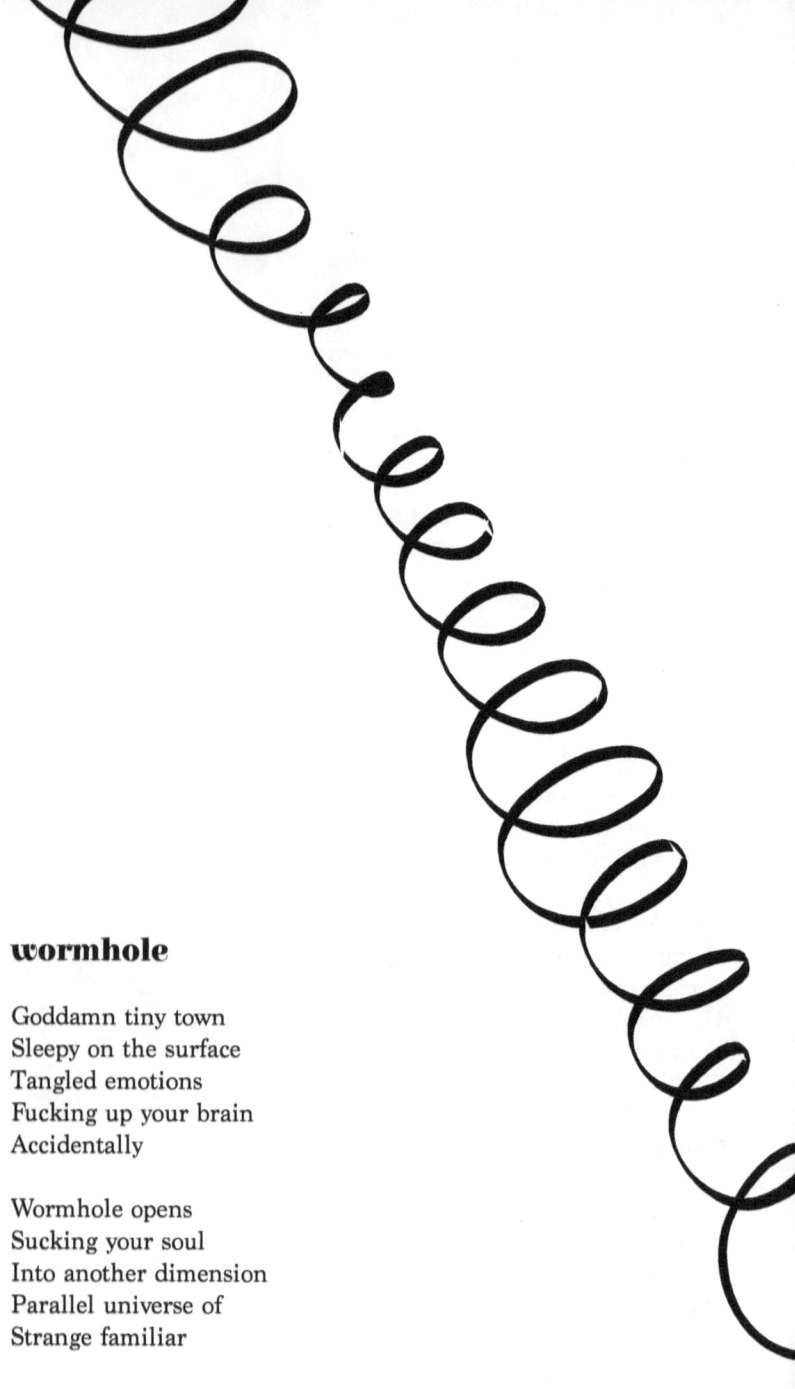

wormhole

Goddamn tiny town
Sleepy on the surface
Tangled emotions
Fucking up your brain
Accidentally

Wormhole opens
Sucking your soul
Into another dimension
Parallel universe of
Strange familiar

tidal marsh

The glory and pain of small towns
is their isolation, the feeling of
remote sleepiness.

They are tidal marshes, teeming
with unique life under a
smooth surface. Quiet, boring,
uninteresting, a pass through or
fly-over zone for adventure seekers.

Low energy zones, where beauty is
subjective, often overlooked.

Their very existence allows for
incredible amounts of diversity, and
yet in so many ways they're exactly
the same as the influences that
formed them.

Salty sometimes, brackish often,
occasionally far too fresh.
It remains open to debate whether
the world at large is formed by
what happens in tidal marshes (and
small towns) or vice versa.

Once considered useless, drained to
the very brink of extinction, and yet
they persist in numbers defying the
fragility and balance they define.

Whitewash

This town is as restless as I tonight.

Sometimes I hate how much I love this tiny place. It'd be so much easier not to care, not to want acceptance.

94% white 10 years ago, and change threatens the status quo.

It wasn't long ago that the sale of alcohol downtown was illegal. Methodist roots run deep, even when no longer tied to the Bible.

Church bells toll every hour, ringing my memory of a little white church on a native reservation — white saviorism inside colonialism.

Sacred brick streets are hallowed by 100 year old maples, learning institutions ancient by Midwest standards, and the passing of ancestral feet and vehicles.

Whitewash as a lifestyle is a given, a matter-of-course ingrained in the seams between the bricks. Social justice is a novel idea, a notion of equality that falls out in easy words.

What does it take to change — truly change? Time and words haven't accomplished it.

Change demands building something new, one brick, one bridge at a time. Construction only comes when demolition is complete.

Fellow white people, we've got a hella lot of demolition to do.

Even in little whitewashed backwater towns too sleepy to protest.

No.

ESPECIALLY here.

covid

Leper
Hiding alone
Glass & walls between
Me, my kids, my friends

Tired
Mildly sick, afraid
Deathly complications
Happen without warning

Anger
Directed my way
Because I'm disrupting lives
I've followed the rules

just words

I'm tired.
Not physically, necessarily. That too.
But so tired of people abusing their power to hurt others.

Tired of words used as weapons.
Of constantly looking for hidden motives.
Guarding my tongue to the point I write anonymously often, and I still watch what I say.

Words are incredibly powerful.
They can hurt or heal.

The power of a platform is not in the elevation ...
It's in the distribution of words.
Reach and impact.
Credibility.

Words have the ability to change behavior.
In individuals.
In groups.
In entire cultures.

They wound.
They bind up.
They give life.
They slay.

I'm frustrated and angry.
There are some people I want to hurt with my words.
They deserve to hurt.
I need to find a way to first do no harm ... and then bind up and heal.

how?

"All these years
I had no idea."

How could you not have known?

Am I so good at hiding
My tears
My fears
My pain?

Am I so good at lying?

How could you not have known?

You saw me
Before
When I was bold and brave
When I faced life head on
And wouldn't quit.

How could you not know?

I was scared
Sad
Exhausted

I changed my whole world
My whole self
To please someone else
And you never knew.

tilt shift

Tilt shift
Edges blur
Sound fades
Single focus

Covid
And cancer
Together
It's not fair

Fuck this
Political shit
Death preys
Undeterred

trust should be earned

You told me humanity can be divine
You told me the feelings I felt were valid
In words I understood and believed
For the first time.
I trusted you.
Trust should be earned, not given
Cherished with gentle hands
Not mocked.

You believed in me when I couldn't believe in myself,
My champion when I had none.
The fact you no longer care,
Or believe in me
Hurts more than you'll ever know.
Today I believe in who I am,
But I no longer believe in you ...
I wish I could.

I wish you knew
How deep your betrayal cut
But that would require acknowledging
The power you've held over me
And I'm too proud
To ever agree to that.
Curse the privilege that binds you
To your narrow window on life
And masturbatory desires.

bravery & fragility

They say I'm brave
Strong
Unbreakable
They're wrong

I'm fragile
Scared
Wounded
Warrior maybe

Just listen
Tell me you care
I need to know
Good exists

Don't try to say
Love wins
Good triumphs
Bullshit

Tell me there's a sun
Bright spots
Warmth
It's enough

Silent

Vulnerability
Transparency
Intimacy

A world, an ocean
Of reasons
To stay silent
Safe.

Dragon Child

She's five today, so I've now spent approximately two and a half years of my waking life wondering whether I'll be able to keep her alive until she's an adult. She's my golden-haired, blue-eyed, dragon-fire-breathing princess. A paper bag princess with messy hair and muddy feet to be sure, but a princess nonetheless. She's the most stubborn person I've ever known besides myself. When she arrives, energy meters burst and people laugh involuntarily.

She takes my breath away daily, and gives it back charged with electricity. She's my life and breath, my heart and soul—she and her sister. The day they laid her on my chest, my heart burst with love for her perfect pudgy fingers and happy snuggles. The day I left her father, my heart shattered at leaving her behind even temporarily. And when she started walking me to my car every night and kissing me goodbye, it took everything in me to leave.

She doesn't understand why I leave. She doesn't understand how desperately I want to keep her with me at all times. She certainly doesn't understand why I can't just live with her father—and yet the sudden drop in conflict in her life changed her dramatically. She doesn't know I leave because I love her so desperately and need her to be safe. She doesn't know I plot and scheme and work myself sick to ensure a future for her and her sister. She does know I love her, and for now, it's enough.

Mirage

Hungry
Bleeding
Invisible

All words I feel in my gut.

Sometimes I think I don't exist. Life itself is a mirage. I crave friendship, allies, closeness. A meeting of minds.

The ability to stand in my own skin without shame or remorse, knowing at least one soul will accept me.

Rotten Teeth and Poverty

I typed the following thoughts on my phone while in the waiting room at a public health "free" dental clinic.

I promised myself I would never live in poverty again, but apparently that is not up to me. Here I am, with my daughter at a walk-in low-income dental clinic, attempting to convince them she needs help with her teeth. And attempting to convince myself not to fall apart. And losing.

My daughter was almost 5, and her teeth were in such a state of rottenness that it was causing her severe pain. Like most dental pain, it was intermittent. My husband was unemployed at the time, and I was making around $1,200/month (working full time).

Before you judge, know that we had moved 3 times that year (counting temporary living that we knew would be a month or so). One was a major cross-country move.

And my daughter has some still un-diagnosed disorders that are fairly invisible on the surface. I mean, she SEEMS normal to most people. But she's sensitive to some normal activities. Tooth-brushing and hair-combing are nightmares.

Add to that a sudden influx of sugar and candy when we moved states due to a daycare with different philosophies than our old one, and dental issues were a given.

I don't want to be here. I don't want some creature at the desk explaining to me how they figure my monthly income (I gave them four months of pay stubs, for chrissake—I know how math works).

I don't like being at the mercy of whatever doctor will see us. I want to pick a good dentist and always see them. I want my girls to have the best of everything—dental care, pediatric care, ballet, violin, piano, sports.

I don't like putting off care until I don't have a choice. I don't like seeing my baby writhing around on the floor in pain from a toothache.

That was one of the most unproductive days I've ever spent. We spent the entire morning at the clinic waiting, and the dentist told me she had at least 3 teeth that needed to be pulled, plus a number of cavities to fill. But he wouldn't do anything at all.

They quoted me a price for service that was astronomical—despite our way-lower-than poverty-level income. Remember, this is the public health dental clinic.

I was eventually able to get my children on Medicaid, although it literally took six months of me prodding the system. My state is not a fan of welfare systems of any sort, and the legislature did not expand Medicaid with the advent of Obamacare.

Meantime, my daughter struggled. I did everything I knew to help her—brushing teeth two or three times/day when she could stand it, rinsing her mouth with a saline solution every night, using Orajel when necessary.

Finally I was able to schedule a dental surgery and get all the issues dealt with at once.
Brushing teeth is still an issue and may always be with this child.

Today we have excellent health insurance, thanks to my husband's job. But why is there no support system for those who are working but still not making enough?

If neither of us were working, we could have qualified easily.

And why is there so much judgment and self-righteousness surrounding poverty? That girl at the desk wasn't making a dime more than me—and yet she could sit there and smirk at me because she had health insurance and I didn't.

Observance

"God isn't real, Mom.
He's not here with us."

It's a statement of fact
Not a question and I...
I have no answers
Let alone words.

She is much wiser than
her five years.

Success

I'm tired of people defining success in terms of big houses, nice cars, dollars. Success doesn't smell like money.
It smells like facing down dragons and winning.
It's wrestling with depression and anxiety and living to tell the tale. Believing something is worth the fight.
Success smells of sweat, mingled with blood & tears.
It's the accomplishment of a soul, and it cannot be measured externally.

Privileged laundry

"If twelve hundred dollars would change your life, imagine what a job would do." I stared at the meme on my Facebook feed, posted by a retired white male who made an upper middle-class wage, and whom I respect in many ways.

I dropped the phone on my bed and went back to folding kids' clothes. Clothes I bought for my kids over the last year, clothes I couldn't have afforded at all two years ago. My mind wanders years back to memories of myself as a pregnant 32-year-old, sick as a dog, unable to get off the couch and drowning in depression knowing there was no insurance.

I had a degree, a full-time professional job, and my husband was working twelve-hour plus days trying to make ends meet. We could barely afford food and our entry-level foreclosure fixer-upper mortgage. Twelve hundred dollars would have bought a full nursery and several months of baby clothes.

I folded some more leggings and thought about moving to the middle of America with a baby and a preschooler. Fighting to get them on Medicaid, watching my five-year-old in terrible pain from a cavity. I was working full time, ten dollars per hour, and so was my spouse. No insurance, no help from the "free" dental clinic. Twelve hundred dollars would have pulled her tooth.

Picking up a shirt with a sparkly unicorn on it, I smile at my youngest daughter's love of sparkly magical things. And then the smile fades, remembering the six months when she was a year old that we lived in an RV park inside a travel trailer with a leaky roof and broken air conditioner. We paid seven hundred dollars per month for the privilege of not living in our car. Twelve hundred dollars would have paid a month and security of rent for an apartment, and literally changed our lives.

I spent over a year washing all the hand-me-downs and grandparent-purchased clothing in laundromats. My parents came through for me in a big way, and I'm eternally thankful for their love. They are not wealthy, but they bought clothes for my kids when they could, shared grocery money, helped with an apartment deposit at one point.

I'm fortunate—very fortunate indeed—to have that slim safety net. I return the love and generosity as best I am able. Folding clothes on the bed in my small duplex, I'm reminded that this too is a privilege, and many do not have easy or cheap access to laundry facilities.

A while back, when I desperately needed a place to call home, my friend loaned me five hundred dollars for a deposit on a living space. I had a job. I should have had money in the bank, equity in my home. But in a time when I trusted no one and was running on fear and adrenaline, that five hundred bucks changed my life.

My life is a crazy quilt of poverty and privilege, loss and love, fear and fulfillment. I am not alone in this crazy. If twelve hundred dollars is not life changing for you—or two thousand, or six hundred—know you are privileged.

Your work ethic does not make you better or special. Your high paying job may be a happy accident due to where you live and who you know.

I've worked since I was nine, first with my parents in their business and then a steady stream of jobs all over the country. No one has EVER said I didn't have a strong work ethic. And still that hasn't kept me from slipping into poverty over and over and over.

I could explain the circumstances of each time. It's not the same old story every time. It's not a lack of foresight, inability to plan, or a need to live above my means. My story is enmeshed with the stories of others and none of us are perfect, all of us struggle with this, that, or everything.

I'm hopeful it won't happen again, but I have no guarantees.

My country—the good old United States of America—is proud of the lack of a safety net. We're proud of our "work ethic" and determined to wear the blinders that let us ignore the immense privilege and wealth keeping so many in poverty and pain. We're uneasy at the thought of shaking up the status quo, because it makes us vulnerable like everyone else.

Twelve hundred dollars isn't life-changing for me today. My kids eat fine, have warm clothing I chose for them or they chose themselves, and far too many Christmas and birthday gifts.

When I was pregnant and uninsured AND working two jobs, Medicaid was life-saving. When my kids needed clothing and I couldn't keep up even with three jobs, hand-me-downs were a gift received with unspeakable gratitude.

If I were in a different point in my life today and we had a worldwide pandemic? Twelve hundred dollars would not be nearly enough but still life-changing and life-giving.

If you don't understand how that can be true, step away from your privilege. Take a good look at the laundry you're folding and try to remember a time life was different.
And if you can't? Now is not your time to talk. Just stop.

Feed

I disconnect
dissociate
fall asleep
zone out.

He sucks my energy
vampire-ish
to feed his voracious need.

He contradicts
argues
ignores
assumes I know nothing—
even about the dumbest things.
Things I know and he does not.

Frankenstein house

I hate this house.
I hate how it's eating my family alive.
I hate how obsessed he is with it, how he can never think about or see anything else. I hate how he expects me to suddenly become carpenter, demolition expert, and handyman.
I hate how he treats me like the son he wishes he had.
I hate that he minimizes my need to take care of my girls.
I hate that he won't listen to me. Or acknowledge or remember that I told him in the beginning I wouldn't be able to help with this house. I hate knowing we don't even have money to buy a furnace. Or a fridge. Or a stove.
I hate not having a safe place for my kids to play - or even a decent table for them to eat at. I hate not being able to cope.
I hate not being able to cook. Or do laundry, or clean. Or decorate.
I hate this house, like the plague it is.
I hate how he expects me to be so excited about every little detail, when I just want it to work. I want a roof over our heads. I want my husband back. I want my babies' father back. I want my life back.
I hate how he can't see me anymore. How nothing is good enough. The harder I work, the more he wants.
I hate how shot I am. I have no room for me, no margin.
I hate how brittle I am, stretched thin and breaking. I can't put out anymore than I already am, and I can't do everything he wants anyway.
I hate how I no longer feel like he cares about me. Like I have no value except in whatever service I can provide. Like he only needs me so he can feel validated.
I hate the loss of the closeness we've shared this last year.
I hate feeling like my family is shattering, and with it all the

pieces of my heart and soul. I hate this. I hate the advice that put us here.
I hate the messiness of building, the constant trash and dirt.
I hate how I never feel like this house will be safe. Or pass any inspection. I hate feeling like my husband is really bad at this, and at the same time knowing that's not absolute truth.
I hate being tired all the time.
I hate poverty.
I hate marketing myself.
I hate knowing my girls need clothes and not being able to get them. I hate not being enough.
I hate not hearing the voice of God in the midst of the storm.
I hate—so, so hate—not being able to plan ahead.
I hate not being able to go to family reunions.
I hate that I can't afford ballet lessons. Or music. Or soccer. Or anything, really. I hate that our bank account is essentially overdrawn, and I don't know where I'm going to get that money from.
I hate that when I work my hardest, and try to maintain everything and do everything, he
fusses at me for not doing _____.
I hate, more than anything else, that he no longer seems to see me as anything except a means to an end.

Coquina walls

Castillo de San Marcos, the 17th century fort in Saint Augustine, Florida, is built of coquina nearly 20 feet thick in spots. Coquina is soft limestone, composed of sea shell fragments and sediment, pressurized by the waves and seabed into something resembling pumice with sea shells in it. It doesn't seem like it should be strong enough to build a fort that would last for hundreds of years.

Yet it absorbed the impact of cannon balls, sometimes simply swallowing them. Many places, the walls of Castillo de San Marcos still hold their violent secrets of ancient wars fought.

The story of walls built of native rock that seemed weak enough to crumble into dust at the first attack feels relevant in terms of trauma, because those walls stole the weapons of their enemies and appropriated them to masquerade as strength and character.

The walls are protective. But they still hold remnants of ancient attacks that are now part of their very DNA.

Trauma becomes part of us. Untreated trauma looks a lot like personality quirks. They say souls that go through hell on earth come out stronger.

They're wrong.

The souls that survive hell on earth are capable of swallowing the pain and incorporating it into themselves. In the end, they're not stronger. They are the same as they've always been, flexible and resilient but hiding giant cannon balls of pain from the world at large.

blood moon

I want to hate you
Sometimes I try
Don't have it in me
Tell lies and go

Blood moon rising
Heart in my soul
The key to wisdom
Is not my goal

shiny shit

"They" say women desire romance. Flowers, gifts, sweet words.
I don't need or trust that.

I need safety & security.
Relationship that will work through the crap.

Intimacy—knowledge that whoever I am, whatever I reveal, I'm safe.
Fuck romance. That's shiny shit.

weakness

He likes me vulnerable.

I allow him in
Let him see my soul
Show him the truth
That holds me captive.
Waves of grief, trauma
Incapacitating depression.
Then
Intense focus and clarity.

Every time ...
It excites him
To see me weak
Dependent.
When I rise
His anger
Explodes.

Intimacy

I crave intimacy. The ability to be seen for who I am, and accepted as such. Valued even.

For me, the concept of intimacy is not really connected to physical touch. I have a wall 10 feet thick around me, and I despise random hugs. My family can touch me, but even then I get "touched out" very quickly.

I've allowed my body to be used as an emotional pacifier for everyone else for decades, and now I wonder why she's tired and hurting.

I've comforted everyone else—my daughters, my husband, former boyfriends, friends—by hugging, holding, offering sex. No one comforts me.

I've let food fill the emotional comfort gap to a degree. That became obvious through several months of gallbladder pain and avoiding fatty foods out of necessity.

My marriage offers surface intimacy—shared daily life, physical relationship, joint friendships, kids. I knew when I got married there were pieces of my soul he'd never understand.

My husband is utterly brilliant in his own right, but it's a very practical, logical genius with no room for emotion or intellectualism. I love art, music, literature, drama and film of all sorts, excellent food, and humor that is as finely crafted as a bar of the best dark chocolate.

My love of literature is a foreign language. The artistic side of music is invisible or misunderstood. His sense of humor is mainly slapstick.

I thought I would be ok, thought I would be satisfied without sharing all of my soul. He's a good person, a truly good person. He cares about me and about his daughters.

If he could accept me for who I am, without feeling a need for me to conform to his way of thinking on every little thing, I think we would be fine. And maybe we'll get there. If I can learn to verbalize (out loud) the words he needs to hear to understand.

I'm not ok right now. My soul needs to breathe, and she's starving for breath, begging to be seen and heard.

I hold back my thoughts and dreams, my personal desires, because I care about my family. I'm hungry, starving for I'm not even sure what. Burying my true self, ignoring my true needs for decades has reduced me to a skeleton ghost.

My soul craves the ability to stand bare, proud and unadorned before someone who matters and to know I will be accepted fully. Not simply unjudged, but admired and understood.

www.ingramcontent.com/pod-product-compliance
Lightning Source LLC
Chambersburg PA
CBHW020547080526
44583CB00013B/1030